DISCARD

Spirit of the South Shore

By William A. Raia

Dedication

This book is dedicated to South Shore employees, passengers, and to the people who worked so hard to preserve its passenger service.

Library of Congress Card Number: 84-51673
ISBN: 0-911581-03-0
Printed in the United States of America

HEIMBURGER HOUSE PUBLISHING COMPANY
310 Lathrop Ave.
River Forest, Illinois 60305

©Copyright 1984 by Heimburger House Publishing Company, River Forest, Illinois. All rights reserved. Nothing may be reprinted or copied in whole or part without express written permission from the Publisher.

Foreword

The Chicago South Shore & South Bend Railroad, the final remnant of the nation's electric interurban railroads, is held dear to many a commuter and railfan's heart. This smallish 88-mile line, which runs from the Indiana outpost of South Bend, through the northern Indiana industrial complex to Chicago's bustling Loop, is not only a transportation company, but also a viable, working monument, if you will, of the essence of electric railroading in this country. No where else in this land has this type of railroading remained alive. No where else has electric interurban railroading been able to survive, much less make a profit such as does this line.

To a great extent, the region through which it runs is responsible for its survival. Residential and commercial areas, rural landscapes and huge industrial steelmaking plants all blend to keep the South Shore a working railroad. The thousands of people who commute to Chicago's Loop, and the freight traffic the South Shore is able to generate with its on-line industries, combine to add revenues to the line's coffers.

Too, the railroad's management, and the help and support of the Northern Indiana Commuter Transportation District, are significant factors in the stability and growth of the South Shore.

Now under a new corporate banner, that of the Venango River Corp., the railroad appears to be headed for even more successes in the future.

LAST 20 YEARS ON FILM

Bill Raia has captured the South Shore during the last 20 years on film. He has spent hours—days—traveling the railroad to record the photos you see in this book. He has become friends with many of the South Shore employees, and many of them know him by his first name. Bill's photographic skills, his knowledge of railroading (he's an employee of the Soo Line Railroad), and his devotion to documenting the history of the South Shore, make viewing and reading this book even more interesting and pleasurable.

The proud, rich heritage of the South Shore will continue, and commuters, railfans and especially the people of northern Indiana and South Chicago, will for many more years enjoy the transportation conveniences, and that unique entity called electric railroading, that no other part of the country can claim. Long live the South Shore!

Donald J. Heimburger
Publisher

CONTENTS

Foreward 2

The South Shore: a new era for the last interurban 4

Passenger train service

    Randolph Street 6

    Roosevelt Road 8

    18th Street 10

    23rd Street 11

    35th, 59th, 115th Streets 12

    Hegewisch 13

    State Line 14

    Hammond 16

    East Chicago 18

    Ambridge, Gary 20

    Goff 23

    Miller, Ideal 24

    Ogden Dunes, Tremont, Furnessville 25

    Beverly Shores 26

    Pines, Michigan City 27

    Street Running 30

    Michigan City Shops 33

    Michigan City—east, Smith 39

    Rolling Prairie, Hudson Lake 41

    Bendix 43

    South Bend 44

Freight service 47

South Shore sidelights 64

Last run; first run 67

Roster 74

Looking at the roster 76

Acknowledgements 80

Photos in the passenger train section of this book at the front are generally arranged in order from the Loop to South Bend, but not all subheads shown are South Shore stations. All photos not otherwise credited were taken by the author.

The South Shore: a new era for the last interurban

The history of the South Shore began very inauspiciously in 1903 when the Chicago and Indiana Air Line Railway constructed a 3.4 mile street car line between East Chicago and Indiana Harbor. In 1904, the line changed its name to the Chicago Lake Shore and South Bend Railroad and began constructing an electric interurban railroad between Hammond and South Bend with major stations at South Bend, Michigan City and Gary. By 1909, service was extended west to Pullman, on trackage rights over the Kensington and Eastern Railroad. In 1912, the Lake Shore began to provide through service into downtown Chicago with coaches pulled by Illinois Central steam locomotives from Pullman to Randolph Street Station.

Like most interurbans, the Lake Shore operated on a narrow profit margin during its first years of operation. Even with a passenger volume that exceeded $4 million in 1917, and a reasonably healthy carload freight business, Lake Shore owners never made much money. Both passenger and freight volumes began to decline during the 1920's as competition from automobiles and trucks increased. In 1925, the Lake Shore went into receivership and was reorganized into the Chicago South Shore and South Bend Railroad by utilities magnet Samuel Insull. This takeover marked the first dramatic change in the South Shore's fortunes.

Insull immediately began a massive rejuvenation of the rickety interurban, pouring millions of dollars into a construction program that included upgrading the track and roadbed, building new stations and purchasing a fleet of new cars which began to arrive on the property in 1926 and continued to operate in daily service until 1983. In 1926 the Illinois Central Railroad, which had converted to 1,500 volt electric power, granted trackage rights to the South Shore over its line, allowing it to operate trains directly to Randolph Street under their own power. The entire South Shore line between South Bend and Kensington was converted to 1,500 volt DC current for compatibility with the Illinois Central's electrical system.

This availability of through service to Chicago, combined with new, luxurious equipment, expanded schedules and an aggressive marketing program, produced rapid and significant increases in passenger traffic. By 1927, the South Shore increased its schedule to 72 trains a day. The management also established a feeder bus system from Michigan City which at one time operated over 26 routes in three states. The South Shore's marketing department heavily promoted excursion trips to the Indiana Dunes, Hudson Lake and other recreational attractions along the line. Dining and parlor car service was also provided on certain trains between South Bend and Chicago featuring such items as "South Shore steaks" for $2.00. Traffic was up to 3.2 million passengers by 1929 and freight revenues approached $1.6 million. However, the Depression hit the South Shore hard. In 1932, passenger levels were down below 1.5 million and freight revenues had sunk to less than $1 million. By 1933 the Insull empire had crumbled, and in September of that year the South Shore went bankrupt.

The railroad's fortunes quickly bounced back when the company was reorganized in 1933 by Samuel Hart. Under Hart's leadership, passenger volumes increased to 2.25 million in 1941. Gasoline rationing and extraordinary travel demands during World War II produced dramatic increases in both freight and passenger traffic. By 1945, passenger volumes exceeded six million and freight revenue climbed to over $2 million. In response, the South Shore embarked on a car modernization program to increase seating capacity. Thirty six of the cars built in the late 1920's were cut in half and lengthened to increase seating capacity from 48 to 80 seats. The South Shore's maintenance department also installed fluorescent lights and other modern amenities; picture windows and air-conditioning were also installed in 18 of these lengthened cars.

After the war, passenger volumes began to decline, leveling off at about 4 million until the Indiana Toll Road was constructed in the late 1950's. Ridership continued to decline steadily during the 1960's because of stiff competition from the automobile and the increasing unreliability of the equipment.

In 1965, the Chesapeake and Ohio Railroad applied for authority to purchase the South Shore, and in 1967 the deal was finalized. In contrast to the passenger business, the South Shore's freight volume continued to grow after the war. Bethlehem Steel was building a huge steel mill about 15 miles west of Michigan City and this facility, along with the business generated by two coal-fired power plants nearby, held promise for generating sufficient freight business to offset the risks of continuing to operate the passenger service.

In 1971, Chessie proposed a major cut in passenger service levels and increased fares to the Interstate Commerce Commission. In May, 1972, the ICC modified the South Shore's request to cut weekday service from 50 to 28 trains by requiring 39 weekday trains, including only two arrivals and departures from South Bend where the station had been moved from downtown to the western edge of the city. This service reduction and fare increase resulted in further ridership losses, but slowed the passenger deficit.

With operating losses continuing to mount, the South Shore petitioned the ICC to discontinue passenger service on October 27, 1976. The ICC ordered an investigation and hearings were held on the petition in January.

The first real public involvement in saving the South Shore came during these hearings, when various public officials and concerned citizens testified about why the last American interurban should be saved. The ICC ruled that the South Shore should continue to operate passenger service until a final ruling was made.

Out of the abandonment hearings came a grassroots citizen's effort to save the railroad. Two groups, Save our South Shore, and South Shore Recreation, were formed during the winter of 1977 to convince local politicians to provide government funding for the South Shore and to increase public awareness of the importance of saving the railroad. Articles about the citizen effort to save "The Little Train That Could" appeared in the *New York Times* and *Los Angeles Times,* as well as the Chicago and local papers.

On April 7, 1977 the ICC denied the South Shore's abandonment petition and ordered service to be continued for at least 10 months. Also during the spring of 1977, the Indiana General Assembly passed two pieces of legislation. The first bill, signed into law on April 21, 1977 enabled the four Indiana counties served by the South Shore to form a commuter transportation district to operate public transportation across county lines. The second bill created a South Shore Capital Improvement Fund totalling about $3.6 million, made contingent upon the availability of matching funds from the four Indiana counties served by the South Shore and the State of Illinois.

With help from officials of the area's regional planning commission and help from the two citizen's groups, local funds were approved to match the federal funds. Prior to this, each of the county councils involved had already passed the necessary ordinances to create a Northern Indiana Commuter Transportation District. The first official NICTD meeting was held on June 24, 1977 and during subsequent meetings, the NICTD Board of Trustees determined that its foremost function was to develop a capital improvement program to rehabilitate the railroad. A grant application was submitted to the Urban Mass Transportation Administration and approved in 1979. It provided funds to purchase 44 electric multiple-unit rail cars, to rehabilitate the maintenance facilities in Michigan City and all of the electrical substations along the line, and to rebuild the platforms and trackage at Randolph Street in Chicago.

Before the first new rail car arrived on the property on January 27, 1982 the South Shore suffered through several harsh winters which almost brought service to a standstill. The heavy snows which typically blow across Lake Michigan into the Michigan City area played havoc with the aging electrical systems of the half-century-old fleet of interurban cars.

By February, 1983 thirty-six of the new cars had arrived in Michigan City. In April of that year, the South Shore was able to operate 27 of its 34 weekday and all of its weekend trains with new equipment. The final order of eight new cars arrived in Michigan City in July. After these cars were tested and accepted by NICTD, the last regular revenue service train with old equipment was operated on August 27, 1983. The increased comfort and reliability of the new cars produced an immediate gain in ridership during 1983 of nearly 20% over the previous year.

Ridership continued to increase in 1984 and on July 3, daily ridership exceeded 10,000 for the first time in over a decade.

Another major event in the South Shore's history occurred in late September, 1984 when the Venango River Corporation purchased the South Shore from the Chessie System Railroads for nearly $30 million.

John E. Alexander, vice president of marketing for the South Shore, said, "This transaction brings control of the South Shore back to the area it serves. We intend to fully commit our resources and energies to the continued development of the South Shore…and to significantly contribute to the people and economy of northwest Indiana and southeast Chicago."

Venango's purchase of the railroad, combined with NICTD's infusion of public funds, should insure a bright future for this country's last interurban. *John Laue*

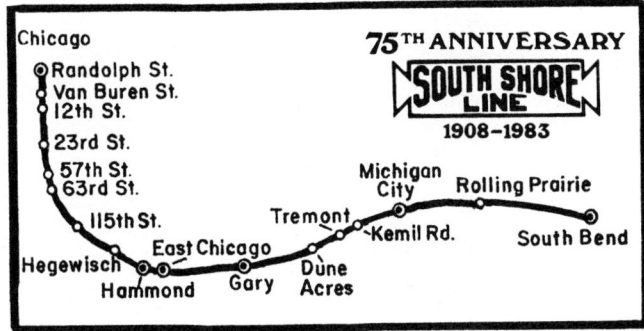

ABOVE. Modernized car 108 stands ready to roll at Randolph Street Station in June of 1950. Car 108 was lengthened in 1943 and received air conditioning and large windows in 1949; car 108 repeated this scene almost daily for 32 more years. *J. Buckley*

LEFT. With Chicago's imposing Michigan Avenue skyline as a background, Randolph Street is quiet between commuter rushes. South Shore and Illinois Central commuter trains shared station platforms in the early days. Later, the Illinois Central moved its trains below the station level, leaving the South Shore with its own facility.

An express to South Bend leaves Randolph Street Station with package express car 503 in tow. Originally Indiana Railroad car 375, car 503 was rebuilt by the South Shore for express service. South Shore's package express service lasted until the early 1970's. *J. Buckley*

A quiet Sunday afternoon at Randolph Street Station finds a two car train just in from South Bend. Shortly, the controlling ends will be changed, and car 15 will lead the consist back to South Bend for another round trip.

The date is Friday, February 18, 1983, and car 24 is ready to lead the last 5:10 p.m. "hot shot" of old cars to South Bend. On Monday, February 21, the train will consist of new stainless steel cars.

Passengers stream down the Randolph Street Station platforms toward the windy city in a scene that is the lifeblood of the South Shore. *M. Raia*

LEFT. The Michigan Avenue skyline lights up the night sky as a one car local waits for an Illinois Central Gulf train to clear. It's cold this December night, but it feels good to be on 109 heading home.

Roosevelt Road

BELOW. On a quiet Sunday morning in July, 1969, car 107 brakes to a stop at Illinois Central's Roosevelt Road Station. To the rear is Chicago's Grant Park and the prestigious Conrad Hilton Hotel on Michigan Avenue.

A six car Michigan City train brakes for the IC's Roosevelt Road Station with nicely maintained car 21 in the lead. In the background Chicago's skyline is changing.

Approximately 10 years later, car 21 is on another Michigan City train in the same location, and like the changes in the Chicago skyline, change will soon overcome car 21 and her sisters as all will be retired within two months.

RIGHT. Accelerating slowly through the maze of switches after discharging passengers at the Roosevelt Road Station, this Chicago-bound Gary local is but one stop away from its Chicago terminal. *M. Raia*

18th Street

BELOW. South Shore train 307 for South Bend passes a Canadian-bound Soo Line freight #943 running on ICG trackage.

LEFT. A mid-day Michigan City local clatters past the IC's suburban train yard at 18th Street on its way south. *L.F. Gerard*

ABOVE. After slowing for the S curve under the IC main line at 23rd Street, the 3:15 p.m. train for Gary rapidly accelerates past prestigious McCormick Inn.

23rd Street

LEFT. On a hot, muggy August day, inbound train 21 overtakes a modern ICG electric which has just stopped at 27th Street Station.
M. Raia

35th Street

RIGHT. A three car Gary local begins to hit its stride after leaving the congestion of the Chicago terminal. Gary is eight stops and 40 minutes away. *M. Raia*

59th Street

BELOW. Shortie car 7 and a modernized combine race past IC's 59th Street Station while an IC local pulls in on the outside track. *M. Raia*

115th Street

BELOW. Heading for home rails, car 108 rattles across the IC main at Kensington. From here to the Indiana border, the train travels over the Kensington & Eastern Railroad built by the IC in 1909 to connect the two railroads and leased to the South Shore ever since. *M. Raia*

Nightfall comes early in this late winter scene at Hegewisch as train 21 stops to discharge passengers.

ABOVE. "Winter on the South Shore." The temperature at Hegewisch is below zero and it shows. Cold and snow are no strangers to the South Shore as its line follows the heavy snow belt of northern Indiana.

BELOW. Short car 34 leads a lengthened car past Burnham Yard on a very cold January 1, 1970.

ABOVE. Train 114 rattles across the Calumet River bridge in November of 1982. This modern bridge replaced an old swing bridge in the late 1950's.

ABOVE. On a hot July, 1979 morning, passengers board a rush hour train for Chicago at Hegewisch, while the conductor confers with the station agent. *M. Raia*

State Line

NEXT PAGE. Just across the Indiana state line, the South Shore runs through the back yards of Hammond. In this idyllic scene, train 315 runs eastbound through the area known on the South Shore as "The Gardens." *L. Hastman*

Hammond

Hammond, Indiana, is one of the major stops on the line and is the first stop eastbound in Indiana. East from Hammond, the Northern Indiana Commuter Transportation District (NICTD) funds passenger operations, while west of Hammond the Regional Transportation Authority (RTA) funds passenger operations. From 1904 until 1909, Hammond was the end of the line for the interurban. In 1909, the final link was completed to connect with the Illinois Central suburban main line at Kensington.

RIGHT. Passengers alight at Hammond Station into much warmer temperatures than the scene below. Hammond, Indiana, is well known for its many railroads, but at this date, only the spunky South Shore provides daily passenger service for Hammond residents.

BELOW. Train 320 brakes to a squealing stop at Hammond Station on a cold, frosty January, 1970 morning. Note the short pedestrian crossing gates.
L. Hastman

ABOVE. The lights begin to flash, the gates lower and auto traffic comes to a halt. A minute later, a familiar orange Chicago-bound South Shore train comes to a stop — a scene motorists have long been accustomed to.

ABOVE. On a hot July, 1968 day at Hammond, a two-car train with air conditioned cars rolling into town provides a most welcome sight to the passengers sweltering on the platform.

BELOW. An overnight heavy snow has turned northwestern Indiana into a winter wonderland, and this South Bend to Chicago train is slightly off the advertised as it races past the B&O CT interchange track just east of Hammond Station.

ABOVE. The date is September, 1943, World War II is being played out, and the South Shore shows its patriotism with car 100 painted in a red, white and blue "Buy War Bonds" scheme. The paint scheme is only one of two different schemes ever applied to South Shore cars. *R. Gibson*

East Chicago

BELOW. Little Joe 802 rolls a short freight through downtown East Chicago, Indiana. The new bypass will be in operation soon, and this scene will be a memory, much to the happiness of East Chicago residents and the railroad. *J. Buckley*

LEFT. Borrowed IC cars roll down the street in East Chicago, Indiana, during World War II. The South Shore often borrowed IC cars when its own cars ran in short supply. *R. Gibson*

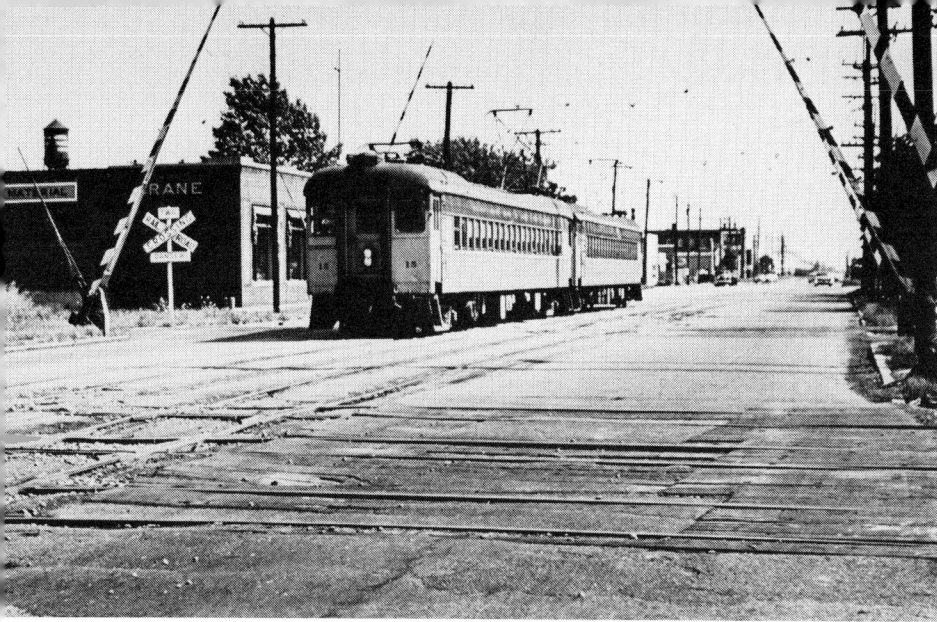

LEFT. In a typical interurban scene, car 15 slowly begins to pick across the Indiana Harbor Belt crossing at East Chicago, Indiana. When the crossing gates go down, South Shore trains have to stop and wait—just as auto traffic does! *J. Buckley*

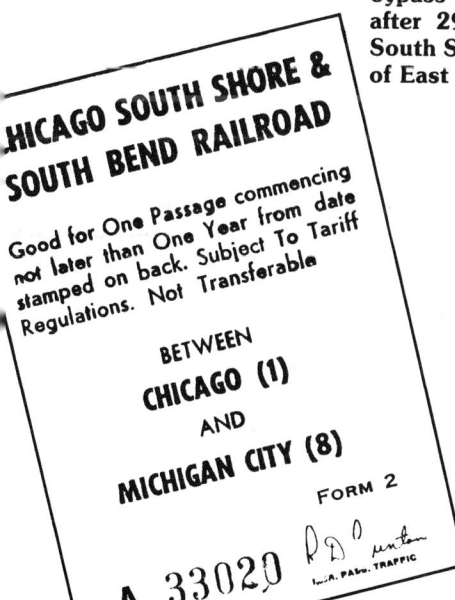

RIGHT. This is today's South Shore at East Chicago. Car 111 heads up a three-car Michigan City train, racing semis along the Indiana Toll Road. The East Chicago bypass became a reality in 1956 after 29 years of trying to get South Shore trains off the streets of East Chicago. *M. Raia*

Ambridge

Gary

ABOVE. A way freight is switching at Georgia Pacific, so this Gary to Chicago local is running on the wrong main. The train is beginning to climb the incline over the Norfolk & Western and Conrail main lines.

RIGHT. On the west side of the Gary Station, these four cars are stored temporarily in the station pocket. Later, these cars may be broken up to make up a Chicago train, or added to other trains.

ABOVE. The year is 1949 and a three car Gary-to-Chicago train picks up speed westward out of the station. In this scene, all three cars still have destination signs in use which were lost to modernization. *J. Buckley*

ABOVE. The motorman has just received two bells (highball) and is notching out his controller past the classic South Shore sign at Gary. Page 20 shows a close up view of the sign. *M. Raia*

BELOW. A Michigan City-bound train has dropped off three cars at Gary. The three cars will be added to car 21 on the left to make up a train for Chicago. All this activity took place within a space of 30 minutes.

BELOW. Two midday trains going in opposite directions pause momentarily at the Gary Station. Gary is the busiest station on the South Shore outside of Chicago. *M. Raia*

RIGHT. Late on a Friday night, car 102 silently awaits its departure with the day's last Gary-to-Chicago local.

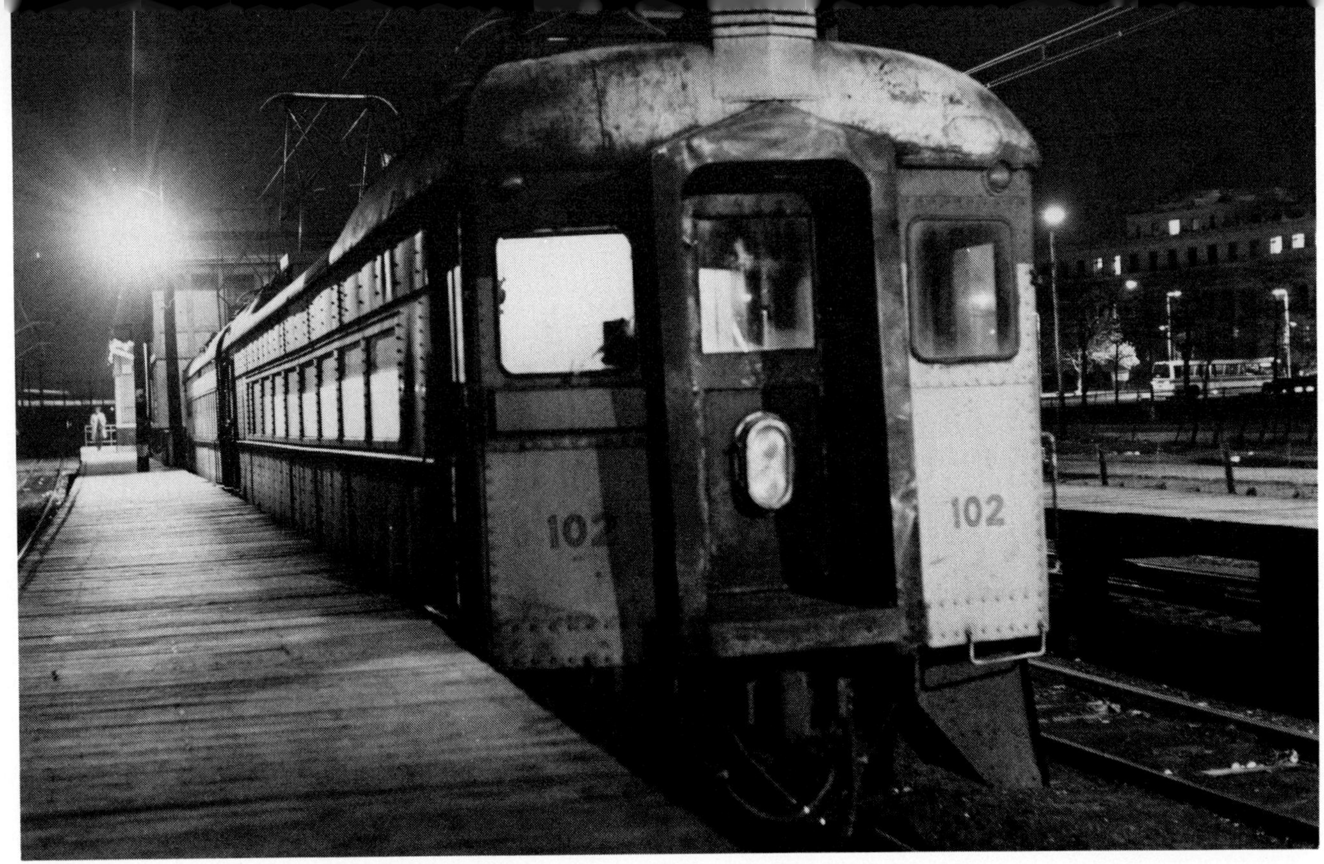

LEFT. A five-car westbound leaves Gary Station as Little Joe 802 looks on. As soon as the morning passenger traffic clears, 802 will head east to the Elgin, Joliet & Eastern interchange at Goff. *M. Raia*

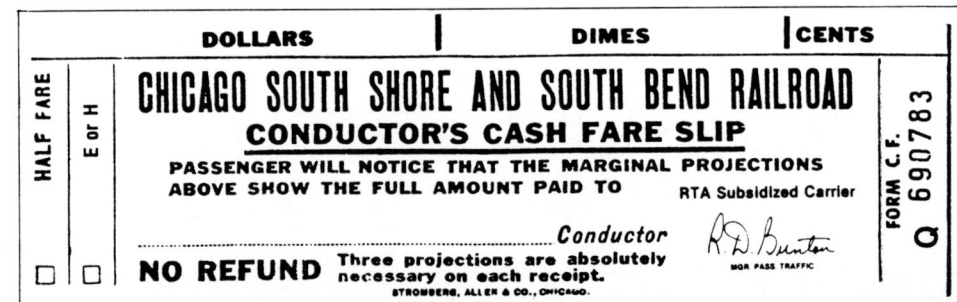

Miller

ABOVE. A two-car westbound brakes down the hill above the Baltimore & Ohio main line into the Miller, Indiana, station. Miller is the site of the main coal train interchange between the B&O and South Shore.

ABOVE. A westbound train highballs through the Ideal section near Miller. This section of double track was Samuel Insull's 1925 reconstruction showpiece. It was patterned after the North Shore's Skokie Valley route and was to be the prototype for the rest of the South Shore. *M. Raia*

Ideal section

RIGHT. A single-car, Michigan City midday train takes the east switch back to single track at Wagner siding, also known as the Ideal section.

Ogden Dunes

ABOVE. Train 305, with new ballast underneath, rolls along in dunes country just west of Ogden Dunes. The Ogden Dunes stop is the first resort stop out of Chicago. *M. Raia*

Tremont

ABOVE. Tremont, Indiana, is the main Dunes area stop. The sign at the left of 108 tells the uninformed which way to South Bend and Chicago.

Furnessville

LEFT. Train 112 passes Furnessville substation. The arrow on the pole at right indicates to the motorman that the controller must be shut off while bridging the gap between substations. *M. Raia*

ABOVE. A single passenger waits trackside for a Chicago-bound train. Beverly Shores is a flag stop where passengers must signal the motorman if they want the train to stop.

RIGHT. This sign in front of the Beverly Shores Station explains to passengers how to stop a train. Beverly Shores is one of 10 flag stops on the South Shore.

Beverly Shores

Beverly Shores Station is unique because it is one of two Samuel Insull stations of Spanish design on the South Shore. The other one, located just west of Michigan City, was known as Lake Shore. The two stations were built to replace four local stops and served as gateways into the resort town of Beverly Shores, developed in the late 1920's by F. Bartlett.

Pines

ABOVE. It's a beautiful winter day as train 109 with car 16 in the lead rolls east through Pines, Indiana, the area formerly known as Tamarack. *M. Raia*

ABOVE. Passengers and express are unloaded from a South Bend train, once a common scene at the Michigan City depot. Car 503 went through two rebuilds, one in 1941 and one in 1952. *L.F. Gerard*

Michigan City

LEFT. Passengers hurry toward a Chicago-bound train at the Michigan City depot. Momentarily causing an auto traffic jam, passengers board the train from the street—so typical of interurban railroading.

BELOW. Long after South Shore bus service had ended and the barber shop had closed, this old sign painted on the rear wall of the depot still recalls busier times at Michigan City.

ABOVE. Night has fallen at Michigan City, and an eight car rush hour train is braking to a stop in front of the depot, its last stop before terminating at the shops. *M. Raia*

ABOVE. The motorman on train #20 looks back to the conductor for the highball at Michigan City depot. Train #20 is the last departure for Chicago of the night.

RIGHT. Late on the evening of April 14, 1982, train 25 for South Bend makes a brief stop at the Michigan City Depot. These nighttime trains always seem so lonely, but are usually the ones we remember the most.

In rain, sleet or snow...

ABOVE. The streets have been cleared of last night's lake effect snow, but because of drifted piles of snow, clearances between automobiles and South Shore cars are tight. *L.F. Gerard*

ABOVE, LEFT. In a driving rain storm, train 21 makes a station stop at Michigan City. The intensity of the rain can be seen in the beams of the headlight. Train 21 will drop the last six cars at Shops and then proceed through the storm to South Bend.

BELOW, LEFT. On another rainy night in Michigan City, a five-car late rush hour train calls at the depot to discharge most of the passengers before tying up for the night at Shops Yard.

ABOVE, LEFT. Here's a look back at Michigan City in 1942 in front of the depot with unrebuilt car 108; compare this scene with rebuilt car 108 shown on page 6. Also note the passing track that was in use then. *J. Buckley* ABOVE, RIGHT. The snow melts on this sunny spring day as car 106 squeals through the S curve just east of the depot.

Street running

RIGHT. The motorman blasts a warning signal on the horn to auto traffic as the orange and maroon cars roll down 11th Street in Michigan City. *D. Raia*

ABOVE. A light snow falls as car 109 rolls down 10th Street at the west end of the Michigan City street running section. *L.F. Gerard*

LEFT. The tight curves in the streets of Michigan City are evident as you look out the vestibule of train 303 on 11th Street. *M. Raia*

NEXT PAGE. The grand interurban tradition is alive and well on tree-lined 11th Street in Michigan City as rebuilt combine 110 heads eastward.

Michigan City Shops

ABOVE. Line car 1100 rests in the old car shop between runs.

The Michigan City shops is where the South Shore maintains its fleet of equipment. It's here where the dedicated employees in later years performed minor miracles to keep the old cars going. Across from the shop complex is the headquarters building; the executive offices are located here as well as the dispatcher's office.

ABOVE LEFT. On a cold December 30, 1982 night, a lone passenger waits at Shops Yard Station for a westbound to Chicago. *M. Raia*

LEFT. Overview of the old shop building where running or light repairs are made to the cars.

A look inside the old shop at Michigan City reveals a variety of equipment receiving running repairs. *L.F. Gerard*

Nightfall at Michigan City finds most of the fleet in the storage yard awaiting tomorrow's call to duty.

RIGHT. A two-car train is readied for service next to the new shop building. At left is the wheel track where sets of new wheels are kept in case a defective one is found and has to be replaced. *L.F. Gerard*

RIGHT. The shop's storage yard is full between rushes. Cars are swept and inspected for defects. In the morning, the yard will empty and another rush begins.

BELOW. Lineup in front of the old car shop. Bar car 203 must be chartered, as the sign in its window indicates Special Party Car. *L. Hastman*

Inside the old car shop are the tools of the trade for repairing the South Shore fleet. The board on the wall keeps orders for repairs to be done.

BELOW. Shopmen are beginning to lower a car body onto a rebuilt wheel assembly, commonly known as a truck. Rebuilding the truck usually entails installing new wheels and reworking traction motors, a job also performed at the Michigan City Shops. *L.F. Gerard*

ABOVE. Standing on the ready track at Shops are "Little Joes" 801, 802, and 803 and car 25 waiting assignment on April 25, 1975.

LEFT. Short motors 1 and 7 have just been cut off a train from Chicago. It is December 30, 1982, and this night marks the end of the line for the shorties—all were withdrawn from service thereafter.

If a passenger walked forward in an old orange car and looked out the front door, he could see the motorman with his hand on the controller, the air brake handle directly in front of the motorman, and to the left the two-way radio which keeps the motorman in contact with the dispatcher and other trains. *M. Raia.*

After the passenger train cuts in May, 1972 and the resulting patronage decline, the South Shore management wanted something to bring attention to its passenger service, and this slogan was the result. The decal was applied to most equipment on the line.

Car 109 and freight motor 702 stand silent in front of the old shop building at Michigan City, awaiting their turn for repairs.

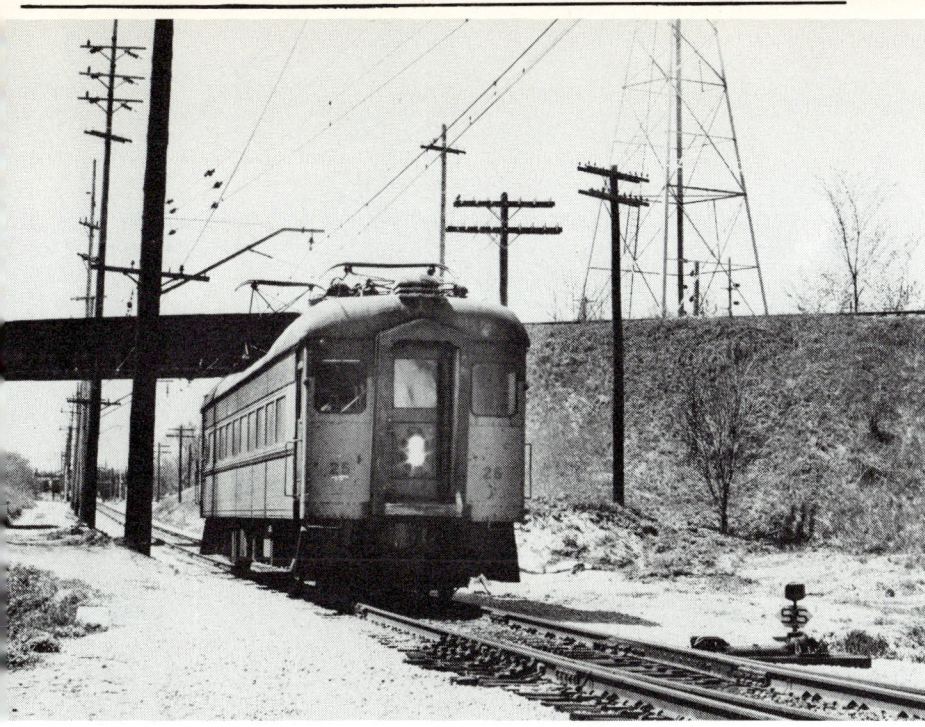

Leaving Michigan City behind, car 25 accelerates under the Chesapeake & Ohio Railroad bridge and heads for South Bend in August of 1981. *M. Raia*

SOUTH SHORE LINE

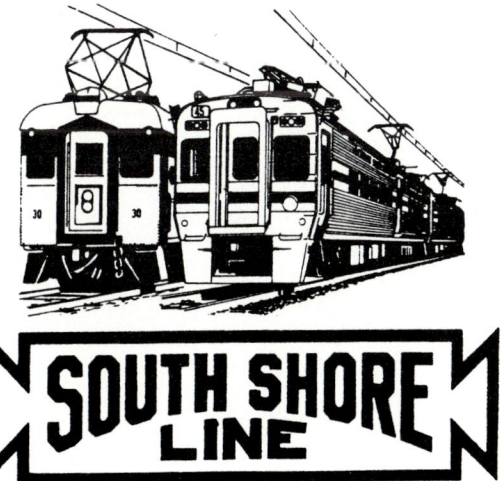

Smith

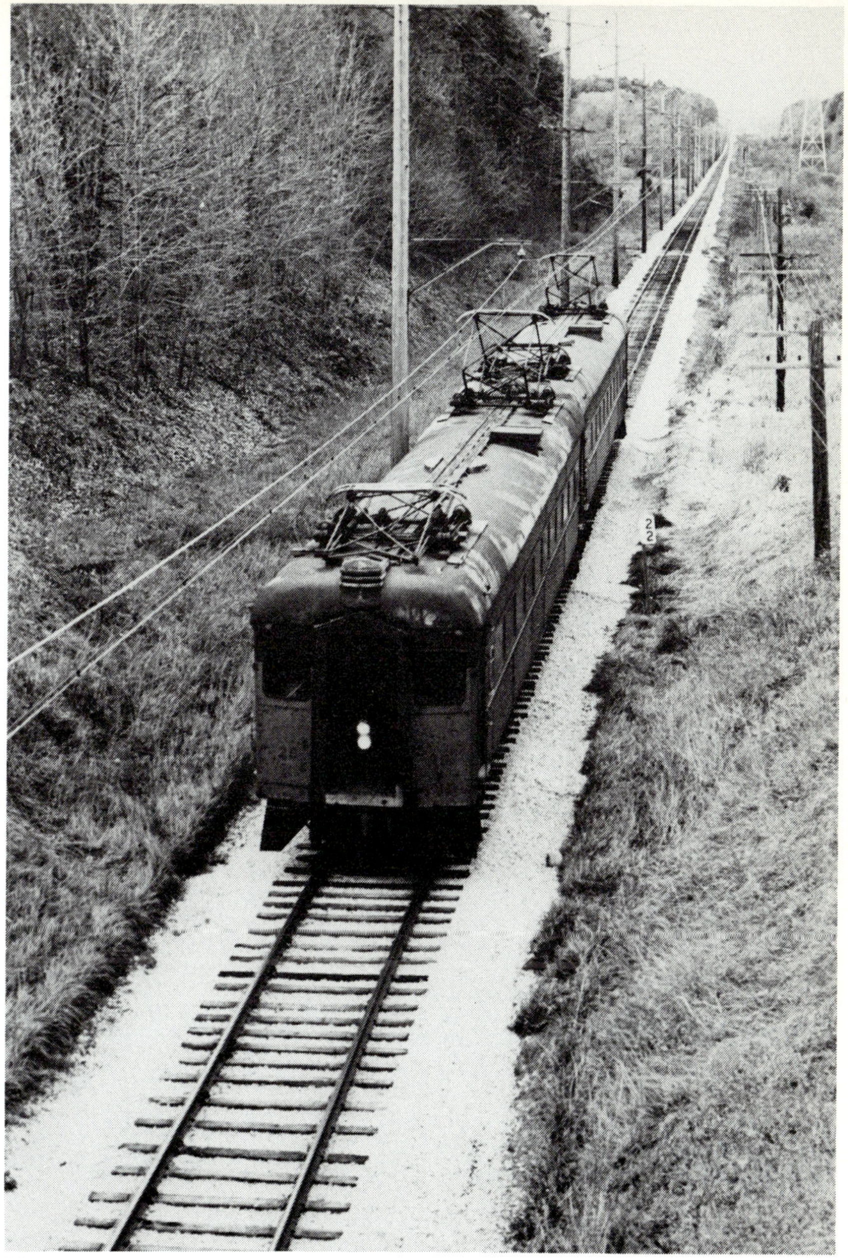

With the controller "on the brass" (wide open), this two-car train races past Mile Post 22 between Tee Lake and Smith, Indiana. *M. Raia*

This quiet, rural Indiana setting is shattered by the sound of train 315's single car racing east at 80 miles per hour. *L. Hastman*

Rolling Prairie

ABOVE. Winter in Sagunay, Indiana! The snow storm has ended, but now car 104 creates its own blizzard in the fresh fallen snow. *L.F. Gerard*

RIGHT. The trolley wire sings as train #303 heads for South Bend through the wooded area just west of Hudson Lake, Indiana. This scenic section is in stark contrast to the industrial west end. *M. Raia*

Hudson Lake

LEFT. A two-car westbound crosses Hudson Lake in a setting that typifies the east end of the railroad. Hudson Lake once was a major stop because of its picnic facilities and dance pavilion where some of the biggest name bands played. *M. Raia*

A timeless interurban scene just east of New Carlisle, Indiana, finds car 104 westbound on February 12, 1972, gliding past grain elevators common to this part of Indiana. *L. Hastman*

ABOVE. Car 24 awaits departure from the new South Bend station at Bendix. The line stopped here when street running ended in 1970. The station is also used by Amtrak, which parallels the South Shore at this point.

BELOW. In August of 1975, car 25 rapidly departs South Bend. Chicago is 88 miles and 2 hours, 5 minutes away. *D. Raia*

ABOVE. Car 107 is just a few minutes from its South Bend terminal on February, 1972. The railroad at left is the ex-New York Central main line operated on this date by Penn Central. *L. Hastman*

South Bend

Car 109 adds to the heavy traffic on LaSalle Avenue in South Bend in September of 1964. It's no wonder why the Shore wanted to escape the main streets of town. *J. Gruber*

LEFT. Two-car train #315 has just arrived from Chicago and is unloading passengers and express on LaSalle Avenue in South Bend. The date is Friday, July 3, 1970, and the end of street running is near. *L. Hastman*

RIGHT. Car 106 crosses the river bridge after leaving South Bend storage yard on LaSalle Avenue. *L. Hastman*

Freight service

RIGHT. The ruggedness and majesty of heavy electric railroading is evident as Little Joe 803 roars around the curve at 130th Street in Chicago during the winter of 1979. *M. Raia*

LOWER RIGHT. In a quieter moment, 803 rests peaceably at the western end of the South Shore at Kensington.

BELOW. An ex-New York Central freight motor heads up a short Illinois Central interchange move at Hegewisch. *L.F. Gerard*

PRECEDING PAGE. Train #320 with car 106 has loaded passengers and shortly will head west through the streets of South Bend for Chicago. *L. Hastman*

ABOVE. Silhouetted against the afternoon sun, 803's impressively large mass is revealed. This rural-looking area is actually still within the Chicago city limits. *M. Raia*

RIGHT. The Calumet River bridge shakes as westbound 803 handles interchange cars for the Illinois Central Gulf at Kensington in March of 1979.

NEXT PAGE. The head brakeman drops off on the fly at the west end of Burnham Yard. After the two head cars are dropped off in the yard, 802 will continue to Kensington.

ABOVE. Another busy day at Burnham Yard! South Shore diesel and electric freight power, and a Belt Railway of Chicago interchange train, line up at the yard's east end.

ABOVE, RIGHT. A pair of 700's are in charge of an Illinois Central pickup from Kensington. These cars will be taken to Burnham Yard and switched out for the east. *L.F. Gerard*

RIGHT. Because of the severe cold, diesel and electric power team up to move a unit coal train out of Burnham Yard in January, 1970.

Heavy electric freight power meet at Burnham Yard on January 2, 1976. No. 802 holds down a main line assignment, while the two 700's switch in the yard. Unfortunately, within four months the 700's would be gone forever. *L. Hastman*

NEXT PAGE. A snowy, cold January day at Burnham Yard finds 706 ready to roll east with a unit coal train bound for the NIPSCO Power plant at Michigan City.

Grinding up tree-lined 11th Street in Michigan City, ex-NYC freight motor 702 leads an eastbound freight towards Shops Yard during August of 1967. *L.F. Gerard*

NEXT PAGE. Geeps 1508 and 615 move a mixed freight past Brunham Yard, headed for the Illinois Central at Kensington in the summer of 1978.

ABOVE. Little Joe 803 switches in Burnham Yard at the Illinois-Indiana state line. After lining up its cars, 803 will double the train to the caboose and head eastward to Gary.

RIGHT. A trio of Geeps wait for the signal to clear at State Line. The unit coal train they have in tow is destined for the NIPSCO plant at Michigan City.

LEFT. A four-unit set of GP-7's begin to pull an eastbound freight train out of Burnham Yard. The diesels were still leased from the C&O as evidenced by the original C&O numbers.

53

ABOVE. Still with their original numbers, four GP-7's round the curve in Hammond with an eastbound loaded unit coal train.

ABOVE. Little Joe 802 is near the Illinois state line with the Gary switch run. Seven cars back are the first two new GP-38 diesels 2000 and 2001 in tow. This day, January 17, 1980, marks the beginning of the end of electric freight service.

RIGHT. A pair of 700's pull up the hill from the Baltimore & Ohio Chicago Terminal interchange in Hammond. The 700's were once a common sight along the South Shore until retired in April of 1976.

PRECEDING PAGE. Grinding through the backyards of Hammond, Indiana, 801 gets the roll on 76 cars eastbound. It's May 10, 1970, and the husky 800's still are assigned to main line freights. *L. Hastman*

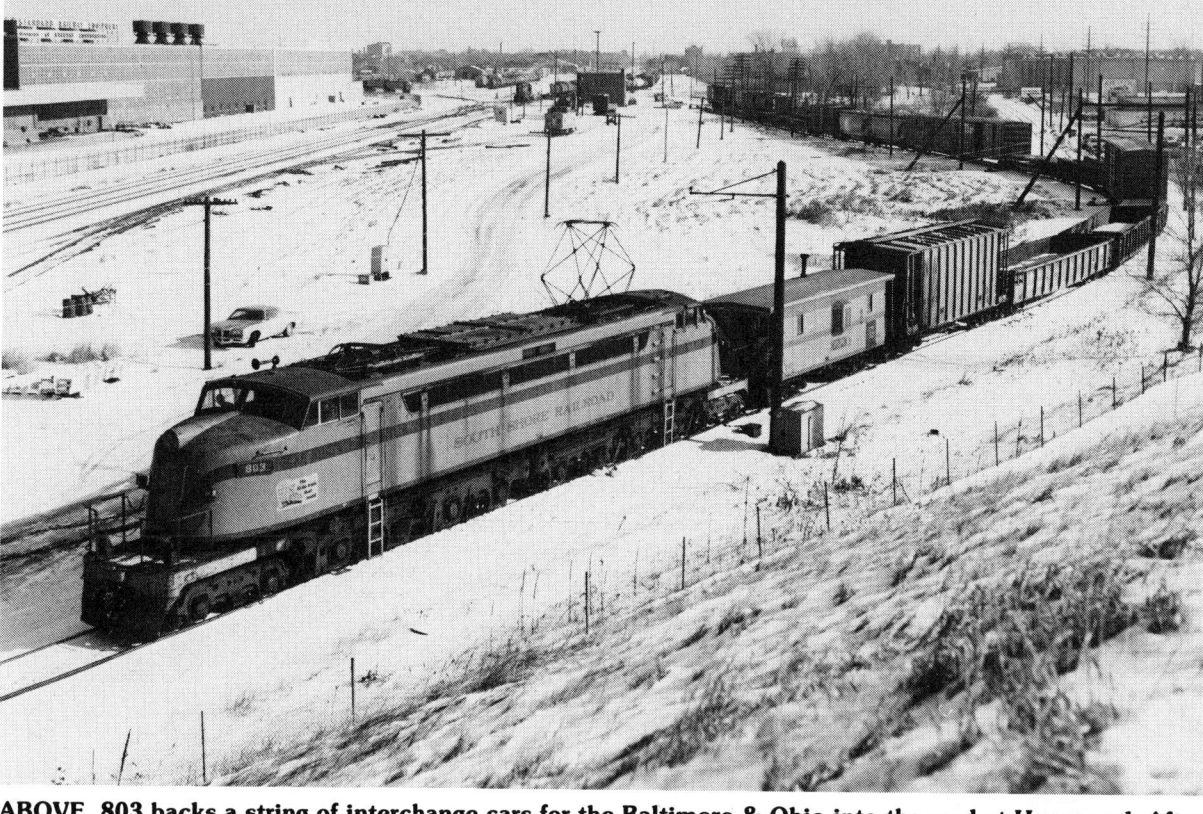

BELOW. Near the end of her career, 803 shows she can still roll the tonnage as she races westward, kicking up fresh snow at East Chicago, Indiana.

ABOVE. 803 backs a string of interchange cars for the Baltimore & Ohio into the yard at Hammond. After delivering the cars, the 803 picks up cars for the South Shore destined for Burnham Yard.

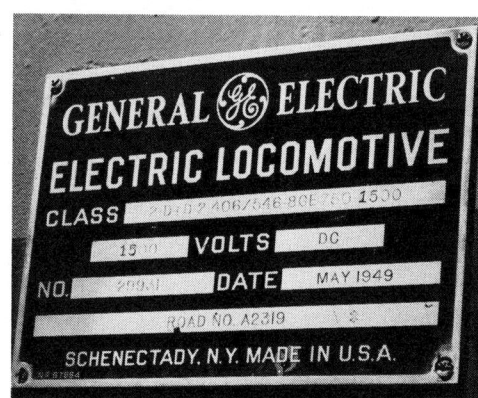

L. Hastman

Northern Indiana Commuter Transportation District

ABOVE. Ex-Florida East Coast diesel 618 comes out of Marshall siding in Gary with the last Gary switch run. One week earlier, 803 ended her career on December 31, 1980, at this location when its brake rigging was damaged on the siding spring switch.

ABOVE. The Georgia Pacific Corporation in Gary, one of the biggest shippers on the line, requires 803 to spend over an hour switching the plant.

LEFT. Pulling into Marshall siding at Gary in the middle of a lake effect blizzard, the crew of this Gary switch job has its hands full with snow-packed switches and little visibility. Just a mile west the sun is shining. *L.F. Gerard*

ABOVE. 803 heads west under the famous South Shore Line sign at Gary station. This picture cannot be duplicated because the Shore now runs on a high fill into the new Gary station, and the sign is part of the memorabilia at the Illinois Railway Museum, Union, Illinois.

LEFT. A crewman pushes up the pantagraph on 802 as it sits at the Gary Yard. Normally the pan goes up without help, but on this cold January, 1978 day it must be prodded into action. *M. Raia*

ABOVE. Two 700's roll an empty coal train toward Burnham Yard past the old Lake Shore Station in January of 1976. The station became a private home and is one of two Insull-designed stations on the line. It was torn down in 1983. *L. Hastman*

ABOVE. A shaggy black dog scampers across a snowy 10th Street in front of 707 which is slowly bringing an eastbound freight into Michigan City. *L.F. Gerard*

BELOW. The conductor of this eastbound freight watches the street roll by as his train threads its way up 10th Street in Michigan City.

RIGHT. The freight trains still roll down the streets of Michigan City and automobiles still dive out of the way, but the "interurban feeling" is now gone from the South Shore's diesel freight service.

LEFT. It's November of 1949 and the Central Electric Railfans Association (CERA) has chartered a fan trip using brand new Little Joe 803 on a regular freight run. Here the train roams 11th Street in Michigan City. *J. Buckley*

LEFT. This is the rear of the same CERA fan trip as above. The trailer was used to haul CERA members at the end of the freight train. Note the steepness of the road. *J. Buckley*

NEXT PAGE. The fog rolls in off Lake Michigan as two 700's prepare to leave the shops for Power Siding where they'll pick up an empty coal train.

South Shore sidelights

ABOVE. The date is April 20, 1976, and all the 700's are standing in Hyman-Michael's scrap yard on Chicago's south side. South Shore's electric freight service was ending.

BELOW. #334 was one of 10 New York Central electrics acquired in 1954 and 1955. It and two others were never converted into 700's, but instead were used for parts until scrapped in 1970. *C. Sennett*

ABOVE. A six-car "borrowed" train of Illinois Central equipment rolls into Gary on July 21, 1946. These cars were used especially on weekends to help with the heavy passenger traffic to the Indiana Dunes. *J. Buckley* LEFT. A rare shot taken June 21, 1975 of a two-car Illinois Central Hi-liner train being tested on the South Shore. This was during the time the Shore was searching for new passenger equipment. *L.F. Gerard*

ABOVE. This unusual looking piece of equipment is South Shore's portable substation. The portable sub is used whenever line voltage is low or a regular substation is being repaired. *L. Hastman*

BELOW. Line car 1100 is in action at Bailly, Indiana. The table or bridge the linemen are standing on swings out from the work car so the catenary over the other two tracks can be repaired. The crew's job is to keep the catenary tight and in good repair.

ABOVE. A Chessie inspection train moves down Wagner siding on October 28, 1983. The train, which included a track geometry car, toured the line to South Bend and returned to Chicago.

During the severe winter of 1982, the fleet of old cars were failing faster than the shop forces could fix them. An emergency limited schedule was instituted, and two diesel powered six-car push-pull trains were borrowed from the Regional Transportation Authority.

TOP, LEFT. RTA F40 104 heads up a train on 11th Street in Michigan City. BOTTOM, LEFT. These bi-level RTA cars are being pushed by diesel power toward Chicago at Michigan City. ABOVE. RTA 104 races through heavy snow at Hudson Lake, Indiana, toward South Bend. All photos, *M. Raia*

Last run; first run

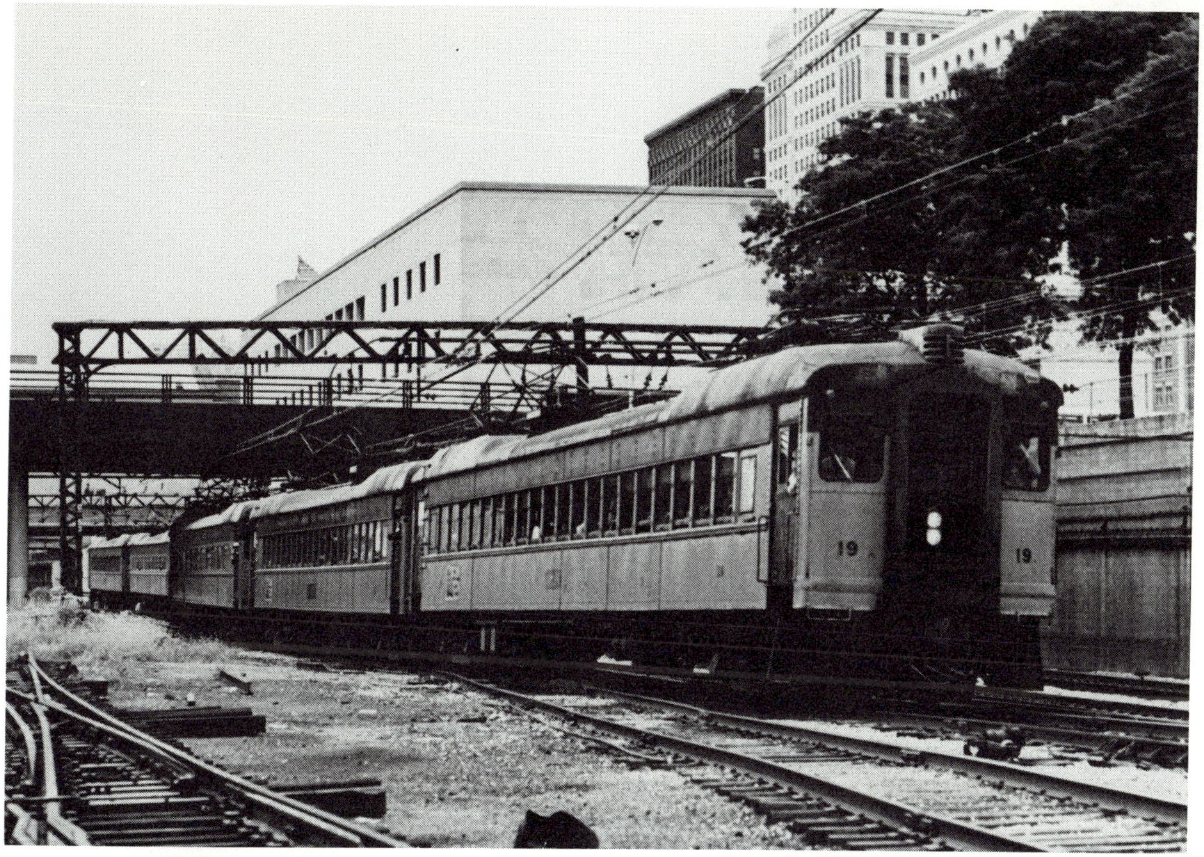

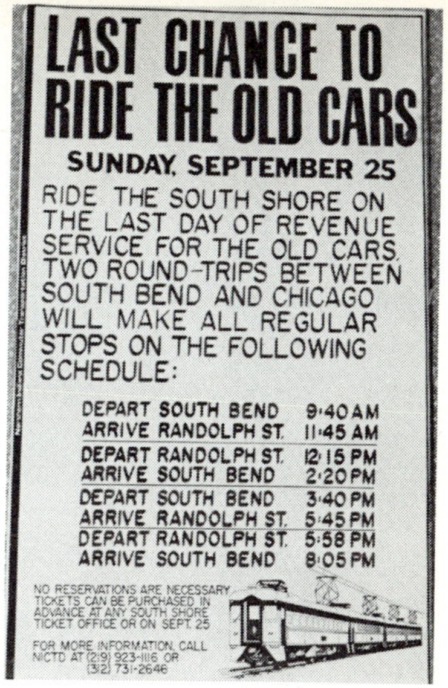
LAST CHANCE TO RIDE THE OLD CARS

SUNDAY, SEPTEMBER 25

RIDE THE SOUTH SHORE ON THE LAST DAY OF REVENUE SERVICE FOR THE OLD CARS. TWO ROUND-TRIPS BETWEEN SOUTH BEND AND CHICAGO WILL MAKE ALL REGULAR STOPS ON THE FOLLOWING SCHEDULE:

DEPART SOUTH BEND	9:40 AM
ARRIVE RANDOLPH ST.	11:45 AM
DEPART RANDOLPH ST.	12:15 PM
ARRIVE SOUTH BEND	2:20 PM
DEPART SOUTH BEND	3:40 PM
ARRIVE RANDOLPH ST.	5:45 PM
DEPART RANDOLPH ST.	5:58 PM
ARRIVE SOUTH BEND	8:05 PM

NO RESERVATIONS ARE NECESSARY. TICKETS CAN BE PURCHASED IN ADVANCE AT ANY SOUTH SHORE TICKET OFFICE OR ON SEPT. 25

FOR MORE INFORMATION, CALL NICTD AT (219) 923-1116 OR (312) 731-2646

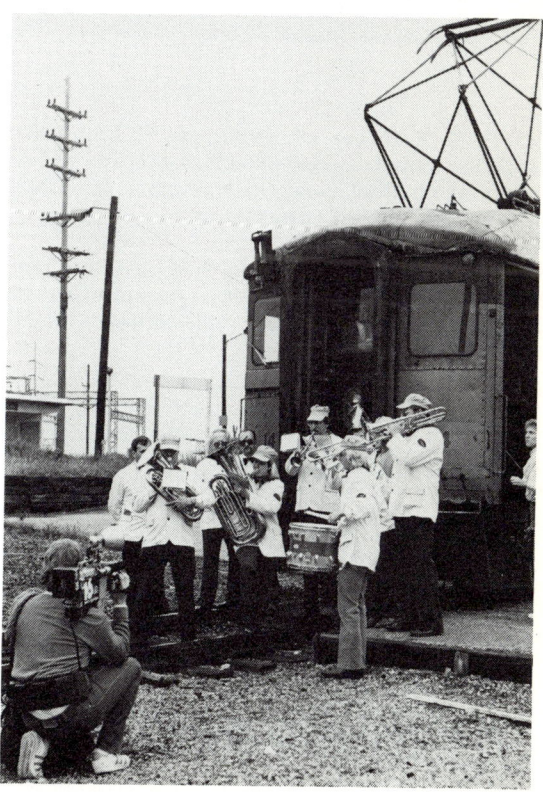

ABOVE. Car #19 brings in the next to the last Chicago arrival of old cars on Sunday, September 25, 1983. This was the last day to ride the old cars, as the six-car set took over two regularly scheduled Chicago to South Bend roundtrips. The last regular service of old cars was on August 26, 1983. *M. Raia*

ABOVE, RIGHT. The sign tells the story. They were posted all along the railroad; about 2,400 people rode the cars one last time.

RIGHT. At South Bend, the 20th Century Railroad Club band plays a farewell just before departure of the last run to Chicago.

NEXT PAGE. Sitting side by side at Randolph Street Station are two generations of interurban cars waiting for the evening runs to begin in March of 1983.

ABOVE. On October 23, 1982, car #1 broke the dedication ribbon at Hegewisch as the first set of new stainless steel cars. Officials gave speeches and a band provided entertainment.

RIGHT. The first set of new cars rolls past Burnham Yard, heading for dedication ceremonies at Hegewisch. An hour and one half earlier the cars were dedicated at Michigan City.

ABOVE. A view of today's modern South Shore as a two-car train ascends up the incline toward the East Chicago Station which was the last great line improvement, the relocation of the East Chicago street trackage. *T. Raia*

ABOVE. Extra 2005 east is in the siding at Goff waiting for train #109 to pass. This is the new South Shore!

RIGHT. Cars 25 and 31 sit in the shops at Michigan City waiting for inspection. Note the RTA emblem on car 31's front door, as cars 31 to 36 are owned by Chicago's RTA system. *J. Smith*

NEXT PAGE. Train #114 with car 4 in the lead roars down the incline over the Elgin, Joliet & Eastern tracks in East Chicago on a hot September, 1983 day.

LEFT. The date is November 22, 1982 and the first afternoon rush hour revenue run of new stainless steel cars stops at Hegewisch to discharge passengers. A new era for the South Shore has begun today.

NEXT PAGE. A two-car train of new cars comes off the double track onto the single track main line at Pines, Indiana, located in the heart of the beautiful Dunes country.

RIGHT. A single-car train rolls up 11th Street in Michigan City. When the new cars arrived, it was rare to see a single-car train, but by the summer of 1983 it was a common sight because by then the new cars had proven themselves. *M. Raia*

PASSENGER CARS

NO.	BUILDER	YEAR	WEIGHT	SEATS	LENGTH	NOTES
1-9	Pullman	26	133,400	56	60'	Coaches 1-39, and trailers 201-313, originally had Pullman-style smoking compartment; #1 had smoking compartment removed 1964 with 3/2 seating and 64 seats.
10 (1st)	Pullman	26	133,400	56	60'	Wrecked 1/1/28 at Parsons, IL
10 (2nd)	Standard	29	129,600	48	61'	Rebuilt 1951 to #110
11-15	Pullman	26	147,000	80	77-6	11 and 12 lengthened in 1945; 13 in 1946; 14 and 15 in 1942; 15 in experimental paint scheme.
16-22	Pullman	27	147,000	80	78-6	16-19 lengthened in 1945; 20-21 in 1946; 22 in 1945; 22 rebuilt in 1960 with split windows.
23-25	Pullman	27	153,200	80	78-6	Lengthened in 1947, rebuilt with A/C and large windows.
26-28	Standard	29	153,200	80	78-6	Lengthened in 1948, rebuilt with A/C and large windows.
29	Standard	29	129,600	48	61'	Rebuilt to car 111 in 1951.
30-39	Standard	29	129,600	48	61'	38 and 39 had smoking compartment removed for 56 seats; 36 rebuilt to 3/2 seating 1964 with 68 seats and smoking compartment removed.
40	Standard	29	129,600	48	61'	Originally trailer 213 rebuilt 1938.
100-101	Pullman	26	150,940	68	77-6	Combine with 8'6" baggage compartment, lengthened in 1943, A/C and large windows added in 1949.
102, 104, 105	Pullman	26	150,940	64	77-6	Combine with 11'3" baggage compartment 102 and 105 lengthened in 1944; 104 in 1943, A/C and large windows added in 1950.
103	Pullman	26	150,940	68	77-6	Combine with 8'6" baggage compartment, lengthened 1943, A/C and large windows in 1950.
106, 108	Pullman	26	150,940	68	77-6	Combine with 8'6" baggage compartment, lengthened 1943, A/C and large windows in 1949.
107, 109	Pullman	26	150,940	68	77-6	Combine with 8'6" baggage compartment, lengthened 1944, A/C and large windows 1949.
110, 111	Standard	29	150,940	64	78-6	Combine with 11'3" baggage compartment, rebuilt from coaches 10 and 29 in 1951 with A/C and large windows.
201	Pullman	27	116,600	80	78-6	Trailer lengthened in 1946.
202-204	Pullman	27	116,600	80	78-6	Trailer lengthened in 1947; 203 has modernized interior, and in 1974 had bar installed for special runs.
205-206	Pullman	27	116,600	80	78-6	Trailers lengthened in 1948.
207-210	Pullman	27	97,000	50	61'	Trailer with smoking compartment.
211-213	Standard	29	97,000	50	61'	Trailer with smoking compartment; #213 motorized and renumbered 40 in 1938.
222	Kuhlman	08	55,900	52	52'	Trailer Ex-CLS&SB #104 rebuilt into deluxe coach in 1927; later used as a work car and finally as a newspaper car.
224	Kuhlman	08	55,900	52	52'	Trailer Ex-CLS&SB #106 rebuilt into deluxe coach in 1927, later used as a work car.
301-302	Pullman	27	113,400	24	64-1	Diner with six-wheel trucks.
351	Pullman	27	111,400	24	64-1	Double end solarium parlor car with six-wheel trucks.
352	Pullman	27	111,400	24	64-1	Parlor car with six-wheel trucks.
353-354	Standard	29	92,350	56	61-0	Parlor car rebuilt to coaches in 1938 and 1939.
401	Niles	08	105,700		57-2	Baggage motor rebuilt 1927 from CLS&SB 71.
501	?	16	47,300		46-4	Baggage car Ex-CLS&SB 800.
502	?	?	?		60-10	Baggage car Ex-IC #271 purchased 3-30.
503	St. Louis	26	71,180		61-6	Baggage car, rebuilt 1941 from IRR, 375, rebuilt again 1952 with additional baggage door installed and windows removed.
504	St. Louis	26	71,180		61-6	Baggage car rebuilt from IRR 377. Rebuilt like 503 in 1955.
1100	St. Louis	26	119,700		61-6	Line car rebuilt from IRR 376 in 1947.
1101	Niles	08	11,000		50'	Line car rebuilt from CLS&SB 72 in 1927.
1-43	Nippon Sharyo Seizo, Kaisha. Ltd.	82-83	115,000	93	85'	Car shell built in Japan and completed by GE in Cleveland, OH. Cars 1-30, 37-43 leased from NICTD; cars 31-36 leased from RTA.

LEGEND
CLS&SB — Chicago, Lake Shore and South Bend RR
IRR — Indiana Railroad
NICTD — Northern Indiana Commuter Transportation District
RTA — Regional Transportation Authority (IL)

Car roster compiled by James J. Buckley with additional data from D. Gornstein, F.D. Lonnes, Northern Indiana Commuter Transit District and Chicago South Shore and South Bend Railroad.

PASSENGER CAR RETIREMENTS & DISPOSITIONS

NUMBER	RETIREMENT DATE	DISPOSITION
1	12/82	National Park Service
2	9/78	1/82 to Overhead & 3rd Rail Trolley Museum, Noblesville, IN
3	9/78	1/82 to Overhead & 3rd Rail Trolley Museum, Noblesville, IN
4	7/79	1/82 to Overhead & 3rd Rail Trolley Museum, Noblesville, IN
5	12/82	7/83 to B&O Museum, Baltimore, MD
6	12/82	National Park Service
7	12/82	National Park Service
8	12/82	Illinois Railway Museum, Union, IL
9	12/82	National Park Service
11	8/83	Overhead & 3rd Rail Trolley Museum, Noblesville, IN
12	8/83	Overhead & 3rd Rail Trolley Museum, Noblesville, IN
13	8/83	Northern Indiana Commuter Transportation District
14	9/83	NIRC - Northeastern Illinois Rail Corp.
15	9/83	National Park Service
16	8/83	Overhead & 3rd Rail Trolley Museum, Noblesville, IN
17	8/83	South Shore Mall, Chesterton, IN
18	5/71	Scrapped 1975
19	9/83	Northern Indiana Commuter Transportation District
20	1975	Stripped, still on property 5/84
21	9/83	Northern Indiana Commuter Transportation District
22	9/83	Seaboard RR Museum, Jacksonville, FL
23	9/83	Northern Indiana Commuter Transportation District
24	9/83	NIRC - Northeastern Illinois Rail Corp.
25	8/83	Wisconsin Trolley Museum, N. Prairie, WI
26	8/83	South Shore Mall, Chesterton, IN
27	1975	Stripped, still on property 5/84
28	8/83	East Troy Trolley Museum
30	12/82	Wisconsin Trolley Museum, N. Prairie, WI
31	4/75	1/82 to Overhead & 3rd Rail Trolley Museum, Noblesville, IN
32	12/82	National Park Service
33	12/82	National Park Service
34	12/82	Illinois Railway Museum, Union, IL
35	5/71	Scrapped 1975
36	12/82	Northern Indiana Commuter Transportation District
37	12/82	Michigan City, IN, Sesquicentennial Commission
38	12/82	Boone Scenic Valley RR, Boone, IA
39	12/82	Boone Scenic Valley RR, Boone, IA
40	12/82	National Park Service
100	3/83	South Shore Mall, Chesterton, IN
101	3/83	Overhead & 3rd Rail Trolley Museum, Noblesville, IN
102	3/83	Boone Scenic Valley RR, Boone, IA
103	1976	Stripped, still on property 5/84
104	3/83	South Shore Mall, Chesterton, IN
105	1975	Stripped, still on property 5/84
106	3/83	Boone Scenic Valley RR, Boone, IA
107	3/83	National Park Service
108	1977	Overhead & 3rd Rail Trolley Museum, Noblesville, IN
109	3/83	Boone Scenic Valley RR, Boone, IA
110	1975	Stripped, still on property 5/84
111	3/83	Fox River Trolley Museum, So. Elgin, IL

NUMBER	RETIREMENT DATE	DISPOSITION
201	3/83	National Park Service
202	3/83	Gengnarel Lumber Co., Auburn, IN
203	3/83	Northern Indiana Commuter Transportation District
204	3/83	Northern Indiana Commuter Transportation District
205	3/83	Northern Indiana Commuter Transportation District
206	3/83	Northern Indiana Commuter Transportation District
207	7/72	Scrapped 1972
208	1974	Scrapped 1974
209	12/71	Scrapped 1972
210	1974	Scrapped 1974
211	1974	Scrapped 1974
212	9/72	Scrapped 1972
222	7/41	Scrapped 1941
224	1933	Scrapped 1933
301	11/41	Scrapped 6/42
302	11/41	Scrapped 6/42
351	12/45	Sold Iron & Steel Products to Canada & Gulf Term as #504 Resold 1984 to Overhead & 3rd Rail Trolley Museum, Noblesville, Indiana
352	12/45	Sold Iron & Steel Products to MBA Construction as MX 300
353	9/72	Scrapped 1974
354	1974	Scrapped 1974
401	1937	Scrapped 1937
501	1931	Scrapped 1931
502	10/34	Scrapped 1934
503	1974	Still used in Michigan City for storage
504	1974	Sold 10/75 to private owner, stored at Illinois Railway Museum, Union, IL
1101	12/47	Scrapped 1948

ELECTRIC FREIGHT LOCOMOTIVES
Compiled by James J. Buckley

500's	BUILDER NUMBER				
505	43681	Baldwin WH 7/16 Never used, sold 3/27 St. Clair Tunnel #9175			
506	43682	Baldwin WH 7/16 Never used, sold 3/27 St. Clair Tunnel #9176			

Renumbered 175, 176; 12/49 out of service 9/28/58; scrapped 4/59

700's	GE (BN)	ALCO (BN)	BUILT	ACQUIRED	EX-NYC NUMBERS	OUT OF SHOP
701	11159	68236	12/30	12/54	1208, 308	5/25/55
702	11165	68242	1/31	12/54	1214, 314	10/20/55
703	11154	68731	12/30	7/55	1203, 303	3/23/56
704	11194	68271	6/31	7/55	1243, 343	9/10/56
705	11191	68268	6/31	7/55	1240, 340	5/31/57
706	11192	68269	6/31	7/55	1241, 341	6/11/58
707	11193	68270	6/31	7/55	1242, 342	5/15/68

All sold 4/15/76 to Hyman Michaels for scrap.

	GE (BN)	ALCO (BN)	BUILT	ACQUIRED	EX-NYC NUMBERS
	11169	68246	2/31	10/55	1218, 318 Never used, scrapped 1969
	11185	68262	5/31	10/55	1234, 334 Never used, scrapped 1970
	11186	68263	5/31	10/55	1235, 335 Never used, scrapped 1970

800's	GE (BN)		BUILT	ACQUIRED	RETIRED	
801	29930		2/49	5/10/49	7/79	8/81 to Hyman Michaels for scrap
802	29931		3/49	5/10/49	1/81	8/81 to B&O Museum, Baltimore
803	29932		4/49	5/10/49	2/81	8/81 to Illinois RR Museum

#803 made last run 1/31/81

900's	(BN)	BUILT	ACQUIRED
900 Baldwin-Wh	61046	9/29	4/41 from Iron & Steel Products Ex-IC 10000
901 Baldwin-Wh	61049	9/29	4/41 from Iron & Steel Products Ex-IC 10003
902 Baldwin-Wh	61048	9/29	4/41 from Iron & Steel Products Ex-IC 10002
903 Baldwin-Wh	61047	9/29	7/41 from Iron & Steel Products Ex-IC 10001

All retired 11/65

1000's	(BN)	BUILT	ACQUIRED	RETIRED
1001 Baldwin-Wh	59012	2/26		9/15/55
1002 Baldwin-Wh	59013	2/26		11/10/55
1003 Baldwin-Wh	59019	2/26		10/23/56
1004 Baldwin-Wh	59020	2/26		11/10/55
1005 Baldwin-Wh	57716	4/24	4/27	3/3/41
1006 Baldwin-Wh	57715	4/24	4/27	3/3/41
1007 Baldwin-Wh	60326	12/27		10/25/56
1008 Baldwin-Wh	60327	12/27		10/23/56
1009 Baldwin-Wh	60571	8/28		9/15/55
1010 Baldwin-Wh	60572	8/28		8/23/57
1011 GE	11075	12/29		3/13/67
1012 GE	11076	1/30		3/13/67
1013 GE	11339	11/30		3/13/67
1014 Baldwin-Wh	61473	9/30		8/23/57

#1005 and #1006 were built for Cuba, never delivered. Sold to Iron & Steel Products and resold 12/41 to Niagara Jct. #10 and 11, Ret. 1953, 11 to Cornwell St. Ry. Lt. & Power Co. for parts. #1011, #1012, and #1013 sold to George R. Silcott Ry. Equip. Co., resold to Peco for scrap.

DIESEL LOCOMOTIVES
Compiled by James J. Buckley

NO.	TYPE	EMD NO.	BLT. DATE	ACQUIRED	NOTES
601	SW-1	1026	3/40	10/56	Ex-Buffalo Creek 42; sold 12/75 to Columbus & Greenville 514, resold to Babcock & Wilcox Co.
602	TR3A	10256	10/49	Leased 2/69	Ex-C&O 6501A, 9555 returned to C&O 10/70
603	TR3B	10254	7/49	Leased 2/69	Ex-C&O 6500C, 9556 returned to C&O 10/70
604	TR3B	10258	10/49	Leased 2/69	Ex-C&O 6501B, 9557 returned to C&O 10/70
605	NW2	10384	9/49	Leased 2/69	Ex-C&O 5063 returned to C&O 10/70
606	TR3B	10257	10/49	Leased 8/69	Ex-C&O 6501C, 9553 returned to C&O 10/70
607	NW2	10386	9/49	Leased 11/69	Ex-C&O 5065 returned to C&O 10/70
614	GP-9	17351	9/52	6/78	Ex-FEC 614, sold 3/81 to Dawx Co. 6/81 to C&G 614
615	GP-9	17352	10/52	6/78	Ex-FEC 615, sold 3/81 to Dawx Co. 6/81 to C&G 615
618	GP-9	17355	10/52	6/78	Ex-FEC 618, sold 3/81 to Dawx Co. 6/81 to C&G 618
5704	GP-7	10133	4/50	Leased 10/70	Wrecked and returned to C&O, 1971
5754	GP-7	15260	11/51	Leased 10/70	Wrecked and returned to C&O, 1971
5770	GP-7	15276	12/51	Leased 10/70	Wrecked and returned to C&O, 1971
5796	GP-7	15302	1/52	Leased 10/70	Wrecked and returned to C&O, 1971
1501	GP-7	10140	6/50	Leased 76	Ex-C&O 5716 sold 3/81 to Dawx Co; 8/81 to Keota & Washington; 5/82 to South Central Arkansas RR. '84 L&NW #52
1502	GP-7	10134	4/50	Leased 74	Ex-C&O 5705 6/81 returned to C&O
1503	GP-7	15243	10/51	Leased 71	Ex-C&O 5747 6/81 returned to C&O
1504	GP-7	15270	11/51	Leased 71	Ex-C&O 5764 6/81 returned to C&O
1505	GP-7	17038	10/52	Leased 76	Ex-C&O 5817 6/81 returned to C&O
1506	GP-7	15284	12/51	Leased 71	Ex-C&O 5778 6/81 returned to C&O
1507	GP-7	17286	10/52	Leased 71	Ex-C&O 5839; 6/81 returned to C&O
1508	GP-7	17280	10/52	Leased 71	Ex-C&O 5833; 6/81 returned to C&O

(1501-1508 first were leased from C&O, then purchased 3/76 and renumbered)

NO.	TYPE	EMD NO.	BLT. DATE	ACQUIRED
2000	GP38-2	796333-1	1/81	1/81
2001	GP38-2	796333-2	1/81	1/81
2002	GP38-2	796333-3	1/81	1/81
2003	GP38-2	796333-4	1/81	1/81
2004	GP38-2	796333-5	1/81	1/81
2005	GP38-2	796333-6	1/81	1/81
2006	GP38-2	796333-7	1/81	1/81
2007	GP38-2	796333-8	1/81	1/81
2008	GP38-2	796333-9	1/81	1/81
2009	GP38-2	796333-10	1/81	1/81

Car #1 is the prototype for the South Shore's fleet of 44 stainless steel cars built in 1982 and 1983; they represent the state-of-the-art in interurban transportation.

Coach 40 shown in 1949. This car was originally trailer #213 before being motorized in 1938. *J. Buckley*

Coach 13 shown in 1939 in original configuration with smoking compartment. *J. Buckley*

Combine 108 as rebuilt from a short car in 1943. *J. Buckley*

Coach 13 as rebuilt and lengthened in 1946 from 60' to 77' 6"; seating capacity increased from 56 to 80. *J. Buckley*

Modernized combine 108 just out of the shop in 1949 with large windows and air conditioning added. *J. Buckley*

Coach 15 in the experimental reverse paint scheme which was applied when rebuilt in 1942. *L.F. Gerard collection*

Trailer 202 was lengthened in 1947. Trailers have controllers, but no traction motors. *J. Buckley*

Trailer 212 shows the original look of the trailers. Trailers 207-213 were never lengthened, and 213 became car 40 when motorized in 1938. *J. Buckley*

Baggage and express car 503 right after being rebuilt in 1941 from Indiana Railway Post Office car 375. *J. Buckley*

Diner 301 had six-wheel trucks which were unusual for a traction railroad. *J. Buckley*

Work car 376 is ex-Indiana Railroad combine 376 shown in 1942. Later, this car became line car 1100. *J. Buckley*

351 is a double-end solarium car riding on six-wheel trucks. *J. Buckley*

Line car 1100 was rebuilt from Indiana Railroad 376 above. This view shows 1100 just after rebuilding in 1947. *J. Buckley*

Trailer 353 was originally a parlor car before rebuilding in 1938. *J. Buckley*

1101 is a wooden line car rebuilt from Chicago, Lake Shore & South Bend #72 in 1927 and retired on December 8, 1947. *J. Buckley*

The 1000's were the main freight power from 1926 until the 800's arrived in 1949. *J. Buckley*

The 700's were ex-NYC freight motors, replacing most of the smaller electric freight motors. They were the main freight power until the GP-7 diesels arrived. *J. Buckley*

1004 and 1005, nicknamed Mike and Ike, were built for Cuba but never delivered. They were acquired in 1927 and were sold in 1941. *J. Buckley*

Little Joe 801 is right out of the paint shop in 1949. These celebrated motors were originally built for Russia but were not delivered. The three 800's served from 1949 until 1981. *J. Buckley*

1012 represents the last group of 100's bought new in 1929-1930 and retired in 1967. *J. Buckley*

601 is a 600 horsepower EMD diesel, the only diesel on the roster from 1956 until 1969. This engine mainly was used at the shops. *J. Buckley*

The 900's were ex-Illinois Central freight motors acquired in 1941; they lasted until November of 1965. *J. Buckley*

606 is an EMD TR-36, known as a calf because it has no controls of its own, and it must be mated with a controlling unit or "cow." *L. Hastman*

607 is an EMD NW-2 used with a calf as described above. These units were acquired in 1969 and did not work out well, as all were returned to the C&O by October of 1970. *L. Hastman*

5778 is a 1,500 horsepower EMD GP-7 diesel unit which took over most of the main line freight hauls from the electrics until the GP-38's arrived and displaced all other freight power.

2001 is a 2,000 horsepower EMD GP-38 diesel unit, representing the only new diesels the South Shore has ever owned. The ten GP-38's replaced all other freight power on the system.

Interior of car #15 — the first car lengthened as part of the South Shore's modernization program after World War II. It is one of 18 cars now owned by the National Park Service, which is studying the possibility of using some of the old cars for shuttle service inside the Indiana Dunes National Lakeshore. *John Laue*

The following is a list of the last active cars on the final runs.

8/26/83 LAST DAY OF REGULAR SERVICE

Last morning train from Michigan City to Chicago: 24, 23, 17, 21, 15, 14
Last Chicago to Gary Local: 14, 15, 21
Last Gary to Chicago Local: 21, 15, 14, 23, 17, 28
Last Michigan City train: 28, 17, 23, 14, 15, 21

RAILFAN DAY LAST RUNS 9/25/83

Last South Bend to Chicago: 19, 21, 23, 15, 22, 14
Last Chicago to South Bend: 14, 22, 15, 23, 21, 19
Car 24 was live in reserve at Shops.

Acknowledgements

The author wishes to thank the following special people without whose help this book would have been impossible: James Buckley for the roster and technical information, John Laue for the history, John Smith for his line drawings and NICTD for permission to use them, Dan Gornstein, Joe Diaz, and James Konas for information, Michael Raia and Lou Gerard for help with the captions and Darlene Raia for doing the typing. Thanks also to photographers James Buckley, Lou F. Gerard, Lee Hastman, Robert Gibson, John Smith, John Gruber, Michael Raia, Anthony Raia, Darlene Raia and Carl Sennett for their photos, and a large debt of gratitude to the people of the South Shore Railroad.